A
JOURNEY
TOWARDS
GOD

A JOURNEY TOWARDS GOD

Zina Williams-Sinclair

XULON PRESS

Xulon Press
2301 Lucien Way #415
Maitland, FL 32751
407.339.4217
www.xulonpress.com

© 2020 by Zina Williams-Sinclair

All rights reserved solely by the author. The author guarantees all contents are original and do not infringe upon the legal rights of any other person or work. No part of this book may be reproduced in any form without the permission of the author. The views expressed in this book are not necessarily those of the publisher.

Unless otherwise indicated, Scripture quotations taken from the King James Version (KJV) – *public domain*.

Printed in the United States of America.

Paperback ISBN-13: 978-1-66280-649-0
eBook ISBN-13: 978-1-6628-0650-6

DEDICATION

THIS BOOK IS DEDICATED TO WOMEN WHO HAVE inspired me through my tumultuous years. Thus, these women have aspired me to follow the lead of the Bible and encouraged me to have, not only faith in myself, but in God as well.

As I trudged my way through the jungles of the wild, these amazing women prepared a path before me and the many possibilities that wait ahead.

Although I stumbled many years, I would always find my way back to the top and only to realize it was Him that carried me each time. I dedicate this book to three beautiful women because they were the prize to my eyes. My mother Carrie Killings-Williams, maternal grandmother, Epsie Stephens-Killings and paternal grandmother, Essie Cooper-Williams, were the women who prayed for me when I did not have the strength nor the sense to pray for myself. My mother presented a humble spirit, encouraged me to pray without ceasing and to always love others even when they were not deserving. My grandmothers dedicated their lives to family and knew how to "cry out" to Him daily.

I firmly believe I was cut from a special cloth: strength, power, and most of all, Love all into one. However, the end results were all the same. Inheriting these amazing characteristics are powerful gifts. These women raised families with strong spiritual beliefs and, at times, never knew where they belonged or where they were headed. Like many, they plundered through the many years of roller coaster tragedies to gain a perspective as to where they belonged and what they should do to overcome their lack of trust and faith in God…eventually they figured it out. As such, they were able to survive traumatic facts in their lives and learned to build and maintain a high self-esteem as well as provide strength and motivation to others like themselves. They were looked upon as legends… not for any accomplishments of fame or fortune, but for whom they were and what they stood for. Only years later, I would have to encounter a few tragedies of my own and to later realize the stamina and motivation I possessed, to move forward, was a trait and blessing. These immaculate blessings were passed down

Dedication

from my incredible female ancestors along with years of tears and prayers. For that, I abundantly thank you!

Table of Contents

Fear vs. Faith 1

    A. *The Testing Process*. 1

    B. *Trusting* 8

Spiritual Growth 17

- *A Choice* 17
- *Looking in the Mirror* 23

Continued Growth 31

- *Forgiving: Getting Rid of the Baggage* 31

Dumping the Trash 35

Approval of Others 45

The Existence of Hope 55

Closure 67

Introduction

The simplicities of life are taken for granted at so many levels. We have learned to divulge ourselves in complacency and somehow underestimate God's plan for us. We continue to make ourselves our very own enemies because selfishness, shallow displays, and disgruntle behaviors has allowed us to seemingly forget who has total control. Therefore, this book will attempt to shed light on our spiritual mentality as we take a step back to witness the fullness in God as it unfolds. We are complacent in having control of endeavors, accomplishments, and successes, but fail to glance from the peripheral of our spiritual vision and know that it is He who has control of our greatness as well as our misfortunes.

The purpose of this book is to enlighten the many levels of what we encounter in life and how we should not focus primarily on the journey that He has led us, but the salvation we will gain. Understanding our purpose helps us to gain a better understanding of who we are and if, in fact, we have done all that is pleasing to God, then nothing else seems to matter. Our goal in Christian life is to gain trust in God Almighty, maintain faith, and to never take our focus from Him. After all, God is our only source of assurance.

Patience will be tested as well as our faith, and the journey he prepares is always unpredictable. This is because His time is not our time and our ways are certainly not His. Our lives, as we know it now, are not always in the order that we perceive or visualize it to be. This book will also entail the many journeys I have encountered, how faith, fear and spiritual growth plays a huge factor in facing the overbearing challenges that God places before me. Today, although I struggle with the various conflicts of life and continue to fight the evils placed before me; I will continue to grasp tightly to faith as I take the various journeys ahead.

Fear vs. Faith

THE TESTING PROCESS

When my mother would go through a rough spell, she would always use these phrases: "This, too, shall pass" or "It's all good and I won't say that, it's all God". She speaks so strongly in faith, confident in knowing that God will provide. Hearing those spoken words gave me hope and a high level of faith.

That sounds good, but when we are faced with adversity, are we able to hold on to faith when approached with fear? As a child, I used to say, "If anything ever happens to my parents; I am going to die". I am sure there are some who has spoken those words and discovered either sooner or later, the magnitude of that statement was much exaggerated. Some people are not willing to grasp the logic in faith. Why? Because our ideology of faith is having or needing to know—needing to know when and where it should happen. Thus, the fear, somehow takes control. There is never a scientific reason as to when and why negative things occur in our lives. We patiently accept the circumstance and trust the journey.

However, our flesh is not willing to decipher something we cannot see or touch because faith, at that point, is obsolete. April 2013, I received a disturbing phone call that my father had taken ill. The fear set in and I immediately did what I was taught and that was to pray. When I begin to pray, I later realized that I was praying a selfish prayer. I found myself commanding God of what I wanted and became a dictator to a higher power that I say I trusted and have all faith in. Faith is having to trust God and His will, and I did not do that. My late grandmother used to say, "In the end, His will shall be done". No matter what we want or what we do not want, God was going to have His way whether we accepted it or not.

Later that morning, I received a second call indicating that my father died. The first chain of our immediate family was broken and I, at that moment, could not define the depth of fear and hurt I encountered as well as to comprehend what had taken place at that moment. I realized He [God] was all I had. Of course, my support system included my husband, children, mother, and siblings, but he had control of everything, including the fear I was experiencing. He said, **"Have I not commanded you? Be strong and courageous. Do not be frightened, and do not be dismayed, for the Lord your God is with you wherever you go". (Joshua 1:9)**

Somehow, we become victims to our fears: "I do not deserve this" or "My father should not have died". I had the dumb assumption that God was not to take my father. After all the things I was taught concerning my spiritual growth and how to maintain faith, I was unable to sufficiently gather my spiritual thoughts and faith subsequently became obsolete.

Fear tends to take us to a place of complacency. We are okay in entertaining our self-pity and even get a bit angry for something that only God can control. But, when we have faith, we slowly begin to accept His works and trust the process and journey along the way.

In time, I began to see God's perspective and accepted my father's death, reluctantly, as I am reminded daily that I am no respective person.

I am not in control and problems can occur in my life just as well as the next. Of course, my faith was put to a test because I did not die due to my father's death because God has sustained me, provided strength during my fear, and I always look to the hills when it appears that my dark days are approaching. But how does one get over the pain and defeat of losing someone? It is never an easy task as death has always been a part of God's plan.

We must first, lose ourselves... meaning, we must play by God's agenda and not a strategized agenda made by us or man. His agenda is not negotiated nor can it be improvised. This is where faith comes into existence because we cannot conclude that we can change anything that has been deemed or destined by God. So, when we have lost a love one, did not get the expected job or beautiful car, it is evident that God's motive supersedes our desires, wants, and needs. From these moments, we should be able to gain knowledge, understanding and reasons for God's plan, with any journey at any given time.

While standing in the water, Jesus told Peter to walk towards Him and to focus primarily on Him. I am sure Peter was afraid of the unknown.

In the event, Peter was distracted by the wind and took his eyes from Jesus, which could have resulted to a drowning. But what was Peter's cry out to Jesus? **"Lord, if it is you, tell me to come to you on the water" (Matthew 14:28).** There was some hesitancy in his voice and lack of faith. However, Jesus was able to save him, even after he revealed his lack of faith and stated to Peter, **"You of little faith. Why did you doubt?" (Matthew 14:31)**

When we are embedded or focused on things other than God, we lose sight and faith in Him, who undoubtedly, manages to make ways that no human can possibly do. When the opposing teams, faith, and fear, are against each other, it is always easy to swiftly cheer for fear if we are not sure how to obtain the faith we need. Faith is surety of gaining peace in our lives, having a sanity lifestyle, and surrendering to His will. In addition, faith bans us from being able to maintain control of every situation and to be okay with that. My mother always says, "Our arms are too short" and "God is not pleased that we get in His way". Can you hear God saying, "You need to mind your business and stay out of mine"? All in all, it is okay to not to be okay because our worries and fears are technically a task for God. Some people have a true belief that they have the power to resolve all their fears and heroically believe they have the "I will, and I can do it on my own" mentality until the situation becomes too large. Allowing our problems to become God's, whether the problems are minute or a relatively great size, is one sure way to let go and let God. We do not have the capabilities of choosing which problem we should allow God to resolve, as God will always have His way. The related scripture, **"I can do all things through <u>Christ</u> that strengthens me". (Philippians 4:13).** Take notice, the scripture states through Christ. We cannot wake us up in the morning. As some would strictly believe and give credit to the alarm clock or the children, remember Jesus could not accomplish the miraculous things He did without God. Jesus is our negotiator, the go between, and the spokesperson for us. If God feels it is our time, it is done.

When situations occur that are way beyond our control, we, perhaps, get an "aha" moment and suddenly realize God is what we really need. As we trail this thing call life, we must always remember He is there. We must also remember that God does not give part time blessings and we should never be part time prayers. Faith is knowing he is always with us even when we have stumbled upon fear, He is there… our cushion when we fall and our strength to prevail.

Praying selfish prayers, asking Him to take away whatever our hearts, souls and minds cannot digest, demonstrates selfishness and a total lack of faith. With faith, we must put on the whole armor to protect us from the wiles of the devil. From a military standpoint, before the soldiers go out into the battlefield; they must insure they are equipped with all the artillery needed to defeat the enemy. They are trained to recognize danger that may bring awareness among themselves. As such, they have all their weapons as protectors.

We, also, are soldiers for God and He has given us every religious tool to maintain faith to defeat the enemies. **Ephesians 6:11 says, "Put on the whole armor of God that ye may be able to stand against the wiles of the devil".** This scripture speaks volumes. So, what exactly does that mean? You see, in a physical sense, the military have their protection of weapons but, in our spiritual battle, we have the protection of God…

we have the strength of God and that is all we need. Remember Eve, in the garden? The devil did three things: He questioned and challenged God's word and without doubt, lied on Him. The faith of Eve was undoubtedly foggy as well as her beliefs. As a result, Paul wrote these words: **II Corinthians 11:3 "But I fear by any means, as the serpent beguiled Eve through his subtilty, so your minds should be corrupted from the simplicity that is in Christ".** We are told and warned that there will be things and people that will deter us from righteousness.

Staying focus is difficult especially when we are being attacked by enemies we do not recognize. If we are not totally engrained in the words of God and thus, using prayer as our defense mechanism, we will lose sight of God's command and this will be an open door for the enemies. Troubles will not stop but your going will get easier. God does not forget to give us what we need, and He does not owe us anything. As a reminder, we cannot beat God's giving.

TRUSTING

To be prepared for any trilogy, trials, or tribulations we need to put on the whole armor with a sprinkle of faith. There must not be a reasonable doubt of God's promises. Remember Job? God took everything from Job and even dismantled his body. Job never gave up due to the extraordinary faith he had for his Savior. Without hesitation, Job's wife commanded him to curse God and die. In his depressed state, he continued to trust God, not man, in the process. Faith is the absolute solution to the wars we must face. People will cause havoc in our lives, rejoice in our despair and even lead us in destructive paths, just as Job's wife.

Have you ever been so afraid of a situation happening in your life and felt you had nowhere to go, or so you thought? Many of you have taken the toll of going to a friend or so-call friend to hopefully assist you in solving a situation that neither you nor your friend had any control.

If you have no control of the journey laid before you, what make you think your friend does? What will often happen is that we take matters into our hands and the results are a total disaster. Why? Because we did not trust the journey God planned. Situations, devastations, and crisis will enter our lives when we least expect. But the secret to peace amid any storm is to have belief in God as you trust his will.

Nine years ago, we adopted an eight-year-old boy. He was vivacious, inquisitive, confused, and scared. He had been placed in several foster homes and possibly abused physically, mentally, or emotionally. Adoption, for us, was very scary because of the unknown and the fact that we were informed by outsiders that a large percentage of adopted kids are often troubled kids. Of course, this placed a bad image in our minds but did not hinder our decision to move forward. We wanted to give back and the decision was final. As Christian-minded people, we begin to pray and only ask God to lead us through this process...even if it was not the true plan for us.

After successfully completing the MAPP training and Home Study, we were able to receive the help in finding a match for us. Still, we did not know what was ahead and could not fathom what was about to take place. Immediately, we were matched with this young man who had many questions and problems to boot. He had tendency to lie, steal and be manipulative. His trivial offenses became much larger for us to handle, or so, I thought. Due to his faults, in anger, I wanted to give up. There were even times I would question God's work, but I remembered the time I ask God to lead us... however, I failed to trust His lead many times during this event. My husband and I stayed the course and would often run into despair. But God picked us up and placed us back on the path we were to trail. After many years of hurt, disappointments and tears, today, this 17-year-old has brought tears of joy, happiness, and a sense of sunray into our home. He is musically inclined, very intelligent and obedient. Just as we had to take the journey to get him, our son had to take a journey to gain us. To be without a mother or father, raised in foster homes to face the unthinkable was the journey God deemed for him. He was God's diamond in the rough. Although he could not understand God's plan, He was preparing him for a better outcome.

The world is depicted as a microwavable regime. We want things when we want it and are not willing to wait, or importantly, pray for it. God is not shallow that he is not willing to understand the desires of our hearts: however, his timing to afford us with greatness is ultimately done in His time. "**For still the vision awaits it appointed time; it hastens to the end-it will not lie. If it seems slow, wait for it: it will surely come. it will not delay. (Habakkuk 2:3).**

We are so quick to forget Him when things are going as we plan, but so swift to regain our "aha" moment when we really need Him. As a reminder, the Bible also says, **"Delight thyself also in the Lord: and**

he shall give thee the desires of thine heart. (Psalm 37: 4). If we truly have trust in God, we also learn to gain patience because the blessings He bestow upon you may not come when you expect, but in God's own designated time.

As children, many of the things they desire requires the permission of a parent. Just as we are obedient to our parents is the same way God expects us to reveal ourselves to Him. Whatever decisions we make, big or small, God will have the last word. He says, **"Whatever you ask in my name, this I will do, that the father may be glorified in the Son (John 14:13).**

One somber day, August 2014, I remember getting the devastating news of testing positive for breast cancer. In my mind, this could not be far from a death sentence. When I received confirmation, my mind suddenly began rewinding to how I consoled others who preceded me in sharing the same experience. However, this sounded more profound when the shoe was on the other foot. I was either going to wear those shoes and trust the process or I was going to play the victim and tell God what I wanted Him to do. Fortunately, I had the spiritual sense to trust the process. Of course, the first few miles of this journey, I begin to question the process: When are they going to remove this thing? Why are they taking so long? Why do I have to go through all these testing? And I want it removed and removed now! My trust abilities were fading.

Even if I did not want to wait on God, he promptly revealed to me that he had full control of my crisis and me having a pity party was not going to stop Him from taking me through this journey. I found myself disappointing him time and time again. Later, I had the sympathetic nerve to ask, "Why me?". That question was either stated in silence or at a screeching yell. Although this was a fear I did not want to challenge, God had to remind me that He had the answer to all my future sufferings, and endurance was held by his significant wisdom, in which, again, I had no control. Grueling as it may seem, God made this choice for me and I had two options: increase my faith to a higher level and take this ride or suffocate myself in a deep sorrow. This was a portion of my journey that God mapped out for me… my very own journey that would determine if I really trusted Him.

Although I am in remission today, I reneged on my trust-hood during my therapy. Going into my second week of treatment, my soul began to falter and my mind took me places that God, I am sure, did not approve. As I laid on my couch, I remembered feeling drained, weak, and stricken with fever. For a split second, I did not trust the process that God set before me. I wanted to give up and later I surprisingly shared with my husband that he needed to enjoy my presence for the next two years, as I could not do this anymore. I mentally withdrew myself from the mercy of God and felt it was necessary, at the time, to take full control of my situation. My husband quickly responded, "But you say you trust Him…have faith". Here my body was riddled with a disease far more than the mind can perceive. I saw no end to this despairingly and riveting situation. How could I win this war that He has bestowed upon me? And although my husband's words were true, mentally, I did not process his consoling words. Later that night, I was awakened from a deep sleep, I felt my lips moving, saying repeatedly, "I said I will be with you always". Spiritually, He was reminding me in my sleep that His presence will always be there.

Matthew 28:20 says, teaching them to observe all that I commanded you; and lo, I am with you always, even to the end of the age". I knew this, but my problem appeared more bigger than my prayer in he beginning.

Those words of consolation and confirmation was all I needed to continue the journey God had for me.

Telling God we trust Him only leads to His testing process. In due time, God will place us in uncomfortable circumstances to test the trust abilities and to confirm whether there is truth to our beliefs and whether our beliefs hold to faith. I later remembered **Psalms 46:1, "God is our refuge and strength, a very present help in trouble.**

Faith is nothing we should carelessly barter or use as a convenient tool. With all the uncertainties in the world, faith is necessary as it gives us the certainty we truly need to face the turmoil and many fears.

Furthermore, negotiations have no place in the plans God has for us because he is a just God. Unfortunately, there are no rehearsals set forth to bring awareness of what is to come. Being content is knowing that God is no shorter than His promise. Do know that we must put in the work.

"Work without faith is dead" (James 2:17).

For example, God cannot bless you with a job unless you physically complete the job application. As such, once you make that one step, He will, in time, make the steps necessary for you, but not always the steps you anticipate. Trust is a must and imperative to have when seeking salvation.

Spiritual Growth

A CHOICE

The world, as we know it, is infested with sin. Some sinful acts present no limit. Every human soul who walks upon this earth has been subjected and/or affected by the consequences of sin.

From the beginning, when the world was created, sin made itself comfortable. First, blame and betrayal was conceived in the hands of Adam and trust were of no concern to Eve. When the fleshy needs overshadow the words of God, we have unfortunately, made a very costly decision. True, we are born in sin until we arrive at a marginal decision to seek salvation.

As a child, church and Sunday School was all I knew. But, understanding the logic of attending was not of importance at the time. As the years progressed and I became an adult, I could no longer blame my parents for the choices I made. For they steered me in the right direction, and it was up to me to make a vicarious choice to either continue in that direction or take a detour. Just as God instructed Adam and Eve.

Continuing to attend church services and Sunday School was a choice I had to make. And so, God gave Adam and Eve the same choice in the Garden of Eden: evil or good. Face it, attending church services every Sunday is obviously not a guarantee of getting into heaven; but attending church and Sunday School provides the foundation of how living on this side of heaven should be conducted. In other words, along with the Bible and sermons, received from ministers, it is our map and guidance to how we as Christians, should conduct ourselves to and among others.

During our growth with God, we must allow ourselves to slowly seep into the dark side of things. In other words, we need to experience a few stabs in order to understand the goodness of God. Every soul that has agreed to give themselves to the heart of God, is expected to experience a diversity of sin from all angles. There are times you are going to feel that you have not arrived at the level of God's expectations.

Spiritual Growth

The upside of that is God knows us better than we know ourselves and it is easier for Him to understand we are not perfect and that the flesh will stand in the way.

One summer, I had the opportunity to take my grandson to his doctor's appointment as his parents had to work. Always, before leaving my home, I make it my business to present myself in a positive manner, regardless of what negative thing I am experiencing. I proceeded to explain to his pediatrician that we have reason to believe my grandson has ADD. It was further explained to him what had been observed and so forth. I was expecting him to provide a professional analysis as to what options were available so that we could proceed with the professional help he needed. This doctor immediately began stereotyping. The first question was, "Are both parents in the home?" or "Are there any problems in the home?" I had to digress and consider if these questions were protocol or if this was a huge culture difference due to him being of an Arabic decent. I begin, in my head, justifying his ignorance by thinking there could be either a lack of knowledge in how his culture view the American style of things. He quickly shifts to my middle grandson making a point to say he is behaving like my older grandson and that we must discipline them, his way. Again, I knew I had to trust God to shift my tongue so that my words would not have a lasting effect on my spiritual character. Yes! I was angry at him for criticizing my grandsons and painting a foggy picture of my family values. Had I reacted other than the way God would have wanted me to, this atrocious situation could have created more despicable acts and he would not have been able to see the God in me. To say the least, I maintained my dignity and spiritual mentality.

My first intuition was to take care of the situation in my own way, but I knew it was far too big for me, so I surrendered and left this hurtful event in the hands that I knew was much larger and stronger than I.

However, the positive side to this dilemma is that I knew I had reached the level of pleasing God. I did not get upset, did not retaliate, and I did not dignify his answer with a response. As I walked out the door, I begin to pray for him and myself. Thanking God was all I could do. I thanked Him for giving me the wisdom to conduct my ways in a positive manner and revealing the growth, I had obtained. The true blessings from this episode is that I can forgive him for his insecurities. Judging him was not an option for me and displeasing to God.

At some point in our lives, we lose patience for nonsense as we begin to live for God. As we yearn for His grace and mercy, the most negative and tangibles things of life becomes insignificant and we are able move forward with no regrets. Moving forward means learning who we are, and as I mentioned earlier, knowing our purpose in life. Being truthful to ourselves is the first step in choosing the life that will become pleasing to God and that is allowing others to see how God can and will instill the growth needed to be a humble soldier.

It is amazing how people will condemn others for the many wrong things they have done but will not recognize the growth in that person when they have gained positive patterns in their lives. One, our value, in God's eye is worth more than anything.

Drug addicts, prostitutes and murderers may be in debt with sin, but their lives have value. Yes, they made the choice to be labeled, but they are God's children as well. We are not excluded from making ungodly mistakes and regardless what we do, our sins have been paid. Jesus does not owe us anything and there is nothing in this world we can give Him because he owns us. The only thing He ask of us is to choose the path of righteousness and believe in His word. Let us discuss the book of **Luke 15:1-2**, the parables of the lost sheep.

This story provides a clear understanding that as sinners, God can love them and this scripture addresses the tone:

Now the tax collectors and sinners were all gathering around to hear Jesus. But the Pharisees and the teachers of the law muttered, "This man welcomes sinners and eats with them". Why not? To know the God, we serve, we would have to know that He sees our inner beauty even when our character represents a different perspective. The hatred we exhibit towards one another, the excitement of gossiping about God's fallen soldiers, and the demeaning, yet degrading way others are treated only proves that our spiritual growth is stagnate. There is nothing God would love more than saving souls even if there is only one. For example, the parable of the lost coin has always been near and dear to me.

Luke 15:8-10 reads, **"Or suppose a woman has ten silver coins and loses one. Doesn't she light a lamp, sweep the house and search carefully until she finds it? And when she finds it, she calls her friends and neighbors together and say, Rejoice with me; I have**

found my lost coin. In the same way, I tell you, there is rejoicing in the presence of the angels of God over one sinner who repent

So, you see, even if he has saved all but that one, she will not stop until has saved that one, and He is able to rejoice when He can save that one, that is good enough for Him. However, we must make a conscious decision to love those less fortunate, step out of our selfish circle and be a voice for God. No one is expected to know the Bible from the beginning to the end, but we are held accountable to read the Bible to gain an understanding of His word and make choices that are pleasing to Him. If we are to be soldiers for God, we must be able to educate ourselves sufficiently and spiritually. This is the journey we take when we make the choice to stand as a true Christian.

LOOKING IN A MIRROR

My husband loves the song, "Try Jesus" and attempts to sing it when leading devotion. Try Jesus, He's Alright. What is the content of that song and how does one achieve that goal? Think about it. We do not have a problem <u>trying</u> to amend relationships, <u>trying</u> to achieve a specific goal, or even <u>trying</u> to eagerly cause a disturbance among the people. Here is a choice…<u>try</u> Him. In addition, remembering how far God has brought you or how He has rescued you from some dangerous situations should be an indication that His existence speaks volumes.

Remembering where you were in the past in comparison to where you are now should be evident that God was with you all the time.

From a deeper perspective, we should never downplay our own faults, insecurities or grudgingly ways. Our mistakes and downfalls should be reminders of who we used to be thus, ultimately become testimonies for other lost souls.

My first marriage was a total disaster. I knew, going into the marriage, that he was engaged in drugs, but my thinking was that I can change him. Get it? <u>I</u> can change him. I did not seek God's guidance before marrying because I knew, with all my fiber, marrying this man was going to be the best decision (choice) I had ever made. It was okay in the beginning. But because I did not seek His approval, God allowed me to go through some embarrassing moments. His drug addiction and our damaging finances created an abundance of grief.

Spiritual Growth

My two girls were witnesses to things a child should not be privy to. This was not the plan I had for my family. But this was the plan (mess) I created. Everything about this marriage shouted wrong. My spiritual life was stifling, and my soul was screaming to be saved. I did everything I thought I needed to do to save my marriage, except seek His guidance. I continued to make choices out of the will of God. His willful plan was that He needed me to experience a bit more to get my attention.

My prayers became shorter each day until they became non existence. Finally, when I realized my lack of faith, I suddenly found myself kneeled on my bathroom floor. In my prayer, with the tears streaming profusely, I told God to please take control, use me as He pleases and guide me in the process. After 11years of marriage, God gave me the wherewithal to relieve myself of this union.

After the divorce, blessings began to multiply, I was able to hear God and seek his guidance in my everyday walk. When I see others having to go through the same thing, I saw myself…blame, entitlement, selfishness and greed. I blamed everything on my ex-husband but refused to recognize my part in this as well: demanding of what I needed,

trying to change things and people because I thought I had full control.

This was my mess, my imperfection, and my lack of spiritual wealth. Yes, his choices led our marriage to destruction, but I destroyed my level of faith and decided I wanted to get into the driver's seat. "Walking by faith and not by sight" were not in my plan. It was when I received that "aha" moment and remembered the reasonings of attending church. My upbringing did not leave me; I left my upbringing. The Bible states, **"Train up a child in the way they should go and when he is old he will not depart from it". (Proverbs 22:6)**. I looked in that mirror and knew my soul had been changed and my faith had increased. It was at that period I knew I had to adopt a spiritual system that would keep me grounded before I judge or begin to think I have a perfected life.

Although I am not perfect, I utilize my mirror as a reminder of my growth.

Christians should never exert a negative attitude of judging others because we all have shirked our responsibilities in forgetting where we come from and how God has brought us through some uncanny circumstance. When the notion of judgment takes place, remember to look in that mirror and do some self-seeking and soul searching because God is not done with molding our hearts nor is He done with shaping our train of thoughts. We are still able to make choices, but seek Him, first Have you ever engaged in a conversation with someone who may have experienced some misfortunes in their life…? foreclosure, repossessions and children in and out of jail. During the conversation he/she begin discussing or gossiping about someone else's unfortunate dilemma, when you know they have a few hiccups in their life. As I ponder over this behavior of, what I call, lost souls, I derived at an understanding that most people refuse to look within themselves. I mentioned earlier that we get in our own way and never cease to regulate our feelings and faults or even to decipher who we really are. The unfortunate conclusion to a confused mind is that we get a joy seeing others fail. But do these unsanctified episodes resolve our problems? Never, it pacifies the soul for an intermediate moment.

If we continue to ignore the evil warning signs that are projected, we will never understand salvation. We are stagnating our growth to become someone bigger and neglecting the commands God gives us. In the end we become an enemy and are not in the position to provide spiritual guidance to others.

Before we allow Satan to take full control of our tongue and mind, we must look in the mirror. Each day I look within myself and ask God, "What is it that you have me to do?" or "Have I done all that is asked of me?" We should, at some point, not only hunger for God's word, but grow to live by His teachings provided. Reading the Bible will massage the mind and gives a greater understanding of our imperfection. You will begin to look deeper within yourself…looking in that mirror and noticing your faults, your unacceptable ways and grudging heart. As we notice those biased characters about us, you will begin to see the goodness of God unfold.

As I attended Church one Sunday, I would always witness this young lady's demeanor, who sang in the choir. As the spirit would get high and everyone is praising God in their own way; she would always have a towel and twirl it in the air as her choice of praise. Her joy in praising God would enlighten me. She appeared to have a subtle heart and did not have a problem letting everyone know she loves God. She was not a stranger and would speak to everyone in passing.

One morning I had to attend my child's school and coincidentally, I saw this very same lady at the front office of the school. The office was quite crowded and busy while parents waited to be served. She quickly turned to me and begin complaining about the staff and what they were doing. Out of nowhere, her tongue begins spitting words that was detrimental to the ears. I was shocked!

Why? Because the lady I knew, and saw was praising God in church.

Should I have been surprised? No! She is merely human and does not profess to be perfect. For a short second, I found myself looking into her mirror and forgetting to look into my own mirror. She, too, can make bad choices, I thought.

Ecclesiastes 7:20 says, "Surely there is not a righteous man on earth who does good and never sin"

This event has a two-part dilemma: She never really understood the nature of the what the staff was unable to do nor did she questioned the process. However, her actions presented an ungodly spirit and her patience deemed her as being ruthless. What I observed in the school office was not what I observed in church. We must question our actions before judging the action of others. The moral of this dilemma is that she never

looked into her mirror and never tried to understand her current surroundings.

To grow spiritually is not always easy. There will be times when we must reflect on the mirror…viewing our imperfect ways, praying for less judgment of others and more judging of ourselves. Remember that the mirror begins with us as we are not held accountable of what others do to us, but we are responsible for what we do to others. Lastly, circumstances will make us do things we would not ordinarily do; therefore, we must continue to wear that armor, the protector, the shield, daily to spiritually prepare ourselves of what this life has to offer.

Continued Growth

FORGIVING: GETTING RID OF THE BAGGAGE

We are in the habit of bombarding our minds with a past that causes us pain, hinders our spiritual growth, and makes us unable to have and live a healthy spiritual lifestyle. This, unfortunately, can, not only taint our minds but taint the mind of others you will cross. Let the truth be known, this will lead to an untrustworthy stance from other individuals... walking around angry and displeased with the world constitutes unhealthy relationships with others. What we do or say will affect others, negative or positive, but the negative conjectures will also destroy the spiritual minds. To maintain the spiritual growth that I strive to keep daily, I must continue enhancing my spiritual thinking by reading the Bible. The bible is the weapon and key to a successful growth in addition to keeping our trunks clean. What does that really mean? We will be tested by many as well as betrayed by those who are closest to you. The humbleness in which we hold will slowly fade and our tongues will swiftly regurgitate what the mind forces you to speak. Growth in the spiritual being is not being perfect but will test the true spirit of the flesh. Therefore, we must study His word because the word is, **"Study to shew thyself approved unto God, a workman that needed not to be ashamed, rightly dividing the word of truth. (2 Timothy 2:15).**

We need to know when and what to say to those who go against God and his commands and who will also be willing to test our spiritual warfare. Further, we must set a clear vision on what our expectations are for us and not what others should expect from us. We must also learn to seek the good in people and leave the judgmental aspects to God alone. I expect to treat others with the respect that I look to receive but to also know that others are not going to give you the same respect. I can only be held accountable for my actions.

We tend to exceed our limitations and overstepped our boundaries when we attempt to change others, dislike them for petty reasons and distort their way of life.

Continued Growth

We are not perfect, although some would like to think so, but we are a child of God and all he wants is for us to allow Him to entertain your soul and steer, you in the direction of eternal life. Instead, some of us are holding grudges, busy unloading our filth on the innocent and seeking damnation at every hand. However, we never stop to think how our destructive minds and hearts can cause a domino effect on those in proximity.

The next topic will provide a few facts about spiritual growth and how some things or people can decrease our growth with God.

Dumping the Trash

Anger, jealousy, and hate, from one individual, can bring tremendous pain in another individual's life. For example, my neighbor stopped speaking to my husband and I completely and it became mind boggling. I fretted over this situation a lot and tried to speak to her on several occasions. However, it appeared that I was forcing her speak because her acknowledgements were very cold and bitter. So, I stopped and thought that I would allow whatever was nudging her weary spirit to wear off. Well, today, it has not and the pain I gained from her has not faded away. One day we received a box in the mail and realized she uprooted our sprinkler heads as she said they were in her yard. I became angry and especially at the person that did the work. I was enraged and hurtful because this clearly let me know that she wanted nothing to do with us.

I was deeply appalled and shocked she wanted to hurt us spiritually, mentally, and not to mention, financially. I had to be the better person and not let this get in the way of my spiritual life. I suddenly realized she was dumping her problems on us because it appears, she is not happy within herself.

Thus, it was not for me to carry her bitterness within me because I had no control of her feelings nor her actions. I vowed I would not allow someone to dictate when and how I was to feel when clearly, they are not required nor eligible to make life changes for me. Today, I have let it go but I continue to pray for her and that she will someday release the things that hinders her spiritual growth. As Christians, we should remember that there are people that will be in your cheering corner and some that will not. I have witnessed hate towards me on many levels and quickly learned that it is part of living the Christian life. If I want to continually grow mentally, emotionally, and spiritually, I must accept the good with the bad and continue traveling that road of grace and mercy. It is much easier to love those who love you, but God's test and plan is that we love others who obviously do not love us or mistreat us in some fashion. We are going to be placed in situations that we knew nothing about nor had nothing to do with. In other words, we will get caught in the crossfire for just being there.

We must speak peace in our lives and trust that God will grant us that serenity. As we know, revenge and deceit only set us back and darkens our path to righteousness. I read where someone said, "When you ignore foolishness, it makes the enemy mad". This is so true because anything the enemy come to do; we must give it to God, and he will handle it as he sees fit. Have you ever had an energy that was so high and felt nothing could destroy it? But someone comes along and say or do something to bring it down. I have been there many times. The bible says, **"The Lord's promise are pure, like silver refined in a furnace, purified seven times over (Psalm 12:6)**.

We must put Him first in all our greatness and infirmities. As I grow deeper and deeper into the heart of Jesus, I become to understand the broader meaning of humbleness. I refuse to acknowledge and ponder on the darker spirits of persons that seek attention by hurting others. I continue to praise Him on high and trust that he sees and admonishes the things that will incur sadness and pain within me. At the same time, we must continue to love those who choose not to love respect us and/or decrepit our inability to not love ourselves. We have heard of the old saying, "Misery loves company". If someone's life is miserable, they will do everything in their power to engage in your life to ensure you are not happy. We must be cognizant as to who we choose as an associate or consider friends. The people who support you are often strangers and the people who know you well will, most times, cause emotional harm. Amongst all that negative energy, our job, as a Christian, is to pray and love those who hate you, pray that peace will eventually succumb in their lives and understanding becomes a reality of their behaviors. Once this has taken place, that unhappy person carrying around all that trash will become to understand their ways and repent. How many times have we done and said things that were unpleasing to God? But He continues to forgive us many times over, and although it is not an easy task, it is the strength provided by God that will keep us grounded and humble.

My mistakes and feelings belong to me and it is not righteous to impose my downfalls or mishaps on others. Dumping my inner self on others only makes life to live much harder, for me and the person I am imposing. I am accustomed to trials and tribulations because I see it as a pathway to building me up and making me stronger. The vision we see is different from God's vision. Therefore, I understand that I cannot have everything the way I desire. Getting upset and dumping my problems on others is a continuous distance among the people. We should learn from our mistakes and use them as a reminder of where we were once and how God brought us through. People who choose not to create a bond with our Lord Savior will be forever searching for peace in all the wrong places and causing damnation among themselves. We tend to think that we are in control of every piece of life that God has provided. It is impossible to control and dictate what God had deemed and positioned. We need to make a conscious effort to trust and believe that God is the maker and creator of all things, including ourselves. In addition, when our lives become so disruptive and we feel it is okay to erupt on others instead of God, we are also dumping on people who, perhaps, may be grounded and holds a humble spirit. What do you think the outcome will be? God's ideal plan is to test us on every level, and we must embrace those demons and rebuke in Jesus' name.

ACCEPTANCE OF UNACEPTANCE

A CHILD WILL ALWAYS WANT TO FEEL ACCEPTED by others and strive to fit in with other children...feeling complete and thinking this is the only way to survive or enhance their spiritual being. Think of the many people who are dissatisfied with their weight, appearances, or even the lack of accomplishments. The world has deemed we should look a certain way, what weight size we should be and what we are to do to obtain prestige. Marriages are mesmerized by the false identity of a modeled significant other.

The husband or wife feels their counterpart is not rich or pretty enough. These attitudes of an individual is seeking happiness in places or people that will only place them on a temporary hold of sanctity. Our judgement of others will cloud the true vision of people while tunnel vision inhibits the reality of what is to be seen in all angles of people and things.

As we reach that journey of contentment, we begin to love ourselves and others for whom they are, not for what they have. This sinful world is warped with the idea that we are never to be unhappy and when we are, we gravitate to others, in our circle, to find justifiable reasons as to why certain things happen.

I will not and cannot adopt an inexcusable reason as to why I look a certain way and why I am not rich.

People are not being accepted in, what I would call, a higher standard group unless they meet a certain criterion. This type of stereotyping often leads to depression, heartbreaks and even suicide. Of course, this is the area that we have no control, although we perceived to be, we should look to God to provide healing and acceptance of anything that we did not have control of in the first place. However we look at this, please understand that focusing on His word will keep a lot of garbage out of our back yards.

When I or you relieve us of our trash it affects others, a trend of sorrows and troubled hearts are affected, and the vicious cycle begins. For example, when couples, within a marriage, decide to have extra-marital affairs. When this occurs, everyone loses. She/he exudes their unstable emotions into a home that has accumulated and compounded a vicissitude of problems. This does not resolve or deplete the messy mentality or grudgeful meanings the individual may hold within.

What really happens is that the problems they hold will implode into a catastrophic whirlwind and no one will gain from the effects of the episode.

In the end, the individual will continue to be infected with the following patterns:

Messy
Incomparable
Selfish
Egotistical
Relentless
Abhorrent
Belligerent
Loathing
Egregious

God has placed us all in miserable, uncomfortable place, but that does not constitute us becoming our situation. God wants us to come to him when our burdens are cumbersome and are too heavy to carry. Our responsibility to God is to save others as well as ourselves from destruction and hate. Dump those conceited, selfcentered woes on God. He is the creator of all things... therefore, he can create a clean heart in all of us. **"Create in me a clean heart, O God, and renew a steadfast spirit within me. And do not take Your Holy Spirit from me. (Psalm 51:10-13).**

One, accept God into your life and you will begin to see the goodness he reveals and the peace he restores within your soul. Two, begin to accept and love yourself. You will begin to understand that God created you in his likeness. Acceptance of God and His plans is accepting any circumstance you must face.

Approval of Others

It was never revealed to me that I was to follow the lead of others nor was it ever stated that people always felt they have or had authority over me. Every step in life is a learning experience and we learn, through growth, that people are not going to accept you nor will they will ever approve of your positive steps in life: especially if they simply do not like you for whatever reason. Disapproval of who we are and what we have is the devil's voice of reason as he speaks to us in a loud voice, dictating to us in a grungy, sneaky, and appealing manner are the weapons he possess to sabotage our greatness. The devil forces us to accept things that limits our ability to excel and encourages us to do immoral things that will cause us not to prosper and hinders our spiritual growth.

I remember when I decided to write this book. I knew I wanted to do it but felt I did not have the knowledge or wherewithal to meet the challenge. The devil's disapproval to tell my testimony to others stood in my way for many years telling me,"

You cannot do this," or "This is way out of your league". At times I believed it. But, because of God's greater plan for me as well as His grace and mercy, I was able to allow the power of God to fight the battle of the demon's intentions. God wants us to share with others, minister and help others grow. Thus, God saw otherwise, and the devil was not happy. When we can do things to block the devil's disapproval, I know that we have conquered...it is praising time!

Of course, there are some areas we have no control, although we perceive to think so, we should look to God to provide healing and acceptance of areas we cannot challenge. Once we were created by God, He knew exactly what we would look like, what we would be and most of all the make-up of our inner beauty. So as Christians, we must learn to accept the creatures of ourselves that God has created and love us just as God does.

Closed minds and hearts deter us from having a broader perspective of God and the wondrous things He can do. The mind of the enemy can seep into the hearts and cause havoc within the human body. We are not responsible for the actions of others, but we have a duty before God to steer the trouble souls into the right directions. Will it be easy? Of course, not because some will not believe, and others will not be up the challenge.

We should not entertain people who are not willing to accept us as we are. As an individual, we need no approval from anyone for who God has deemed us to be nor our accomplishments. We have no position to negotiate with anyone of who we are because God has already created the person we are and is to become. Approval of our worth and value is what God sees within all of us. God has chosen us for specific and various reasons. It is not up to any individual to determine if one is accepted in any group, race, or color. **James 2:9** says**, "But if you show partiality, you are committing sin and are convicted by the law as transgressors**.

The world has mocked society to divide humanity which in return has caused disparity and a deep darkness. I get joy in reading this verse, "**I appeal to you, brothers, to watch out for those who cause divisions and create obstacles contrary to the doctrine that you have been taught; avoid them. For such persons do not serve our Lord Christ, but their own appetites, and by smooth**

talk and flattery they deceive the hearts of the naive". (Romans 16:17-18)

There are several things that we should adhere to when it appears that Satan does not approve of what God has deemed us to be: First, we must have common sense, secondly, spiritual sense, and thirdly, the senses and knowledge of His word.

Common sense is a good sense with good judgement in practical matters. It looks and sounds easy, but when sudden situations arise that may distort our thinking abilities, the common knowledge becomes second to none. The evil doers are not content when our souls are at rest and it does not approve of our happiness.

My youngest daughter is very sweet, caring, and attentive to the needs of others. However, she can become a bit "hot headed "when her surroundings are a little uncomfortable and chaotic. She was sharing with me that her supervisor plays favoritism among the employees and does not acknowledge her needs within her job.

She became a bit bitter and quickly said, "I want to quit". She felt that the easiest way, without using common sense, was to retaliate by quitting. I reminded her that she is not responsible for others action; however,

Approval of Others

she is responsible for her own actions and how she treats others and that her sudden actions, without thinking, can cause a major suffering on her part. We react to negative reactions and there is a great cost in the end. **Ephesian 6:12** says, **"We wrestle not against flesh and blood, but against principalities, against powers, against rulers of the darkness of this world, against spiritual wickedness in high places.** I cautioned her to diligently pray, not only for her self, but for those who do not understand their actions. Common sense can lead to greatness and peace of mind.

Then there is the spiritual sense. In time of despair, we tend to fight within ourselves, struggling to solve situations that is so entangled, we do not know where to begin. This is where our spiritual sense should kick in. If we knew every obstacle, we were to face, we would not need God for anything because we would casually resolve the problem ahead of time. Unfortunately, that is not the way it works. God, sometimes allows things to happen as a reminder to us that He is there, all the time. His presence does not warrants His physical being as He listens all the time. In other words, He is a tremendous muliti-tasker. Our spiritual sense comes when we learn to pray to Him, talk to Him and read about and from Him. Our map of life is the Bible. Everything we need to know is engraved in the book. As we grow, we grow spiritually. While we are growing spiritually, we are growing closer to Him. As we grow closer to Him, we learn to use God's radar which speaks to us when trouble or mind-boggling circumstance becomes a challenge. **And we know that the Son of God has come and has given us understanding, so that we may know him who is true; and we are in him who is true, in his Son Jesus Christ. He is the true God and eternal life. (1 John 5:20).**

We sometimes, may have a discerning spirit of those who present an unsettling disposition. However, I have learned, through my spiritual sense, to give them no strong ingredients to build bad images. What do you mean by that? Well, prior to baking a cake, certain ingredients are used. We know that flour, eggs, butter, and sugar are the main ingredients. The basic ingredients give great sustenance which is the strength and nourishment. At the completion of that cake, it is built with such goodness.

On the other hand, when people, poisonous individuals, are constantly giving you words of negativity, tearing you down deceiving you, scandalizing your name and provoking you in every aspect, they are providing the ingredients they will destroy your spiritual strength. By responding, we give them the permission to build an image that God will not approve. We become someone or something that does not go against the wiles of the devil.

Lastly, there is sense and knowledge of His word. **Proverb 2:6** says, "**For the Lord gives wisdom; from his mouth come knowledge and understanding.** To have understanding, we must know and have the knowledge of the word. From time to time, we may engage in religious conversations. However, some people may not agree with your understanding of the bible and tend to misinterpret scriptures (the devil's approval). If our intentions are to guide people in the right path, we must be able to prove to others that His word produces one truth, which means the Bible does not have specific scriptures for specific people. His words are a one size fits all. As we minister to those in need, we must be equipped with the spiritual weapons to fight the demons of the world. In doing so, understand that **2 Timothy 2:15** says, **"Study to shew thyself approved unto God, a workman that needed not to be ashamed, rightly dividing the word of truth.**

Our disposition and mannerism will always be disturbed by some unknown evil spirit because it **(Satan)** will not approve of our happiness and sanity. We are not always going to get the expected approval we desire when the devil has any hand in it.

A bright side to our darken days will eventually surface because God is always there to lend his hand(s). Somehow, we feel there should be a period to our downfalls. We do not hold the period and we, unfortunately, do not have the last say to how our lives should be mapped out for us. So, when the devil intervenes within our homes, jobs or in our relationships, it is a must that we turn to God. When the devil disapproves of our happiness and success, he finds unmeaningful ways to destroy those moments, places negative thoughts in our minds and lead us to total destruction. God, too, can disapprove of the devil's perception that he can conquer a battle between God and His children. So, don't think that when we have escaped death or a terminal illness that it was all your doing. The same God that takes us through the many unfortunate events is the same that will prevent Satan from interfering where he does not belong.

Let us take a stand and see life for what it is. God is our creator and maker of this universe. He holds the one key that (1) Guide our footsteps (2) Protects us from danger seen and unseen (3) Heals us mentally and physically and (4) Can give us eternal life.

The excitement about this key is that it is a one size fits all. No one is eliminated from these guidelines of salvation. Ask yourself, who would you prefer to hold the key to your life... Satan or God?

Remember, God approves of us even when we have disappointed Him, but Satan approves when it is only benefitting to him. God loves us for who we are and will never manipulate our minds into thinking we are nothing less than greatness. There is no secret in what God can do. Our only regret in learning to survive on this side of earth is focusing on the devil and bringing constant confusion in our lives and eternal damnation.

Stop allowing others to give us the stamp of approval because that is the first phase in letting the devil squirm his way into God's plan. Keep in mind that God will disapprove of our infidelities, lies and deceit. In contrast, the devil will approve and encourage us to engage in behaviors that hinders our growth and that, my friend, is the devil's approval.

The Existence of Hope

As a wife, mother, and grandmother, I am constantly in prayer for my family. In reading **2Corinthians 1:8-10**, it reveals that Paul is telling us that these men were aware of their many blessings and when they felt that hope was gone, they suddenly realized who they had to rely on. The scripture reads, **"For we do not want you to be unaware, brothers, [a] of the affliction we experienced in Asia. For we were so utterly burdened beyond our strength that we despaired of life itself. Indeed, we felt that we had received the sentence of death. But that was to make us rely not on ourselves but on God who raises the dead. He delivered us from such a deadly peril, and he will deliver us. On him we have set our hope that he will".**

Our own thinking abilities and way of doing things gets us in trouble and we ultimately fail. For example, we make plans for everything to ensure all goes well and that nothing is not out of place. However, we fail to hold on to hope.

My daughter was preparing her son, my oldest grandson, for school. My family is an advocate for education and ensures that each child is equipped with the things they need. When my daughter decided to place her son in a Christian school, we thought that would be most beneficial. Well, our worries were just beginning. The school's protocol is to provide testing to make sure the child is properly prepared for the next grade. Unfortunately, my grandson did not do very well. The school administrator advised it would be better if he repeated the first grade. My daughter was devastated! She rants and raved and came up with every excuse as to why he should not repeat first grade.

I further explained to my daughter that God is trying to help her understand that preparing him with all the money in the world does not guarantee him understanding the logistics of education; however, God wants us to trust in Him and allow Him to work this out. It may not be what we want, but it's better than what we planned. I explained to her that Jermaine is going to be fine because these weapons the devil has placed before us is not meant to form nor prosper whatever the outcome will be. I told her to trust because God has already deemed this to be an awesome outcome whether he remains in first grade or not.

In my mind, I was well with whatever God's desire to be. I learned to step outside of my vehicle (feelings) and ride with God's. I knew that he would (1) Take my daughter on a journey to test her will and to see if she would lose all hope (2) I knew His will for this would eventually be a greater outcome.

As the weeks progressed, the school called and my daughter and the administrator had the conversation again. It was agreed that they test him for the second time and they did. He did a much better job this time! In the end, they agreed to place him in second grade with academic probation.

WHEN OUR HOPE IS GONE

When our faith begins to fade, we lose grip to the reality of life and feel all hope is gone. But what we fail to understand is that we have an option that is bigger and inevitable than the mind can imagine. Our ultimate and only belief in having hope lies within the power of God.

Disappointments, downfalls, and believe it or not, we are our biggest destruction. When we have the mindset that only our thinking and doing is the only solution to our problems is all we need, failure instantly sets in.

My oldest daughter high school years were closing to an end.

However, as tenth graders, the requirement was they had to pass this test prior to graduating. When she failed the test the very first time, she worried, prayed and kept thinking about the "what ifs". I continued to tell her that she needed to hold on to hope and know that God is in control. I also advised her that whatever path he provided her she was to take that path with a huge leap of faith. As I was giving her the ingredients to maintaining hope, I, myself, begin to wonder if she could do it. In **2Corinthians 8:2**, Paul said, **"In the midst of a very severe trial, their overflowing joy and their extreme poverty welled up in rich generosity"**. I love the theology concerning the birds. **Matthew 6:26 says, "In this verse Jesus tells his followers not to be anxious about food, but to rely on God as the birds, who are worth far less than people are fully provided for".**

Why should we worry for things that God will deliver and ultimately see us through? If the birds are not stressing, and they are no better than we, why should we? If you really think about it, we are the only species that gives God trouble. We make plans for everything: what we eat, wear and even the routes we take in our daily goings and comings. But at what time do we include him into those plans. Hope in God is all we need because his blessings often fill the gaps we are missing.

HOPE WHEN THINGS DO NOT LOOK GOOD

Have you ever just walked the floors in the middle of the night, not knowing what to do in a situation that seems too large for you to handle: losing a job, child gone astray, and losing your home. The prospects of those events do not look good and we feel we have no other option but to give up. Let us look at this from a different angle.

There is a difference between happy and joy. When we have accomplished everything in our lives and it appears that we have conquered the world, we are happy…we have everything we need and want which includes money, big house, fine car and your children and marriage is seemingly running smoothly...that is happy. However, being happy can swiftly sway in another direction and quickly transforms into intense pain and hurt. But when we have gained joy in our lives, we are content with whatever. When death arrives, we maintain joy, when illness surface, we continue to maintain joy. There is peace and solitude within our souls that give us confirmation that we can relax and be content with the worries of this world--joy.

In addition, this is also called that immediate hope. When we have contentment and joy in our life, we immediate turn to him instead of holding on to something that is not ours in the first place.

As a child, we never worried how I parents took care of the things that adults normally do: bills, Christmas, cars. We just knew it was done but we never see what is happening backstage. As a result, we learned to trust that our parents would get the job done.

There are two types of hope: Worldly Hope and Christian Hope. In adopting "worldly hope" we use the words like", I sure hope my child pass this test". But when we carefully look at the "Christian hope" we should clearly understand and should have arrived at the conclusion that Christian hope is based on God's

The Existence of Hope

promises. You can bet everything you have that whatever God says, it is going to happen.

My mother has always been a very strong, independent person.

As they say, "she holds her own". I have never known her to truly depend on anyone, other than God and my dad, to assist her with the troubles of this world. A few months ago, I visited my mother for the weekend to help her with a few financial obligations. When it was time to depart, we kissed and hugged her good-bye and she reminded us to be care and to call her when we had arrived at our destination.

The very next morning, 8:00 am to be exact, she called. Calling that time of morning brings on an alert and concern. I answered and she said, "Yall left without saying good-bye". I was startled. I did not know how to respond. Quickly, I responded, "Mama, remember when we gave you a hug and kissed you good-bye". She was silent for a short time and said, "I thought I heard someone in the back". Now, I did not want to accept the idea that my mother's mind was clearly diminishing. There has not been another episode, but I always find myself trying to control the situation and hope for the best. I am constantly trying to find ways to eliminate her status. Again, I am taking control and attempting to change something that is much bigger that I. In **John 15:11**, it says, **I have told you this so that my joy may be in you and that your joy may be complete**. Therefore, I need to not hold on to my mother's physical thinking, but turn to God with an <u>immediate</u> hopeful heart. If I hold on to the Christian hope, I will begin to let go of all the negative things that life has to offer. With that, I can have joy and peace.

HOPE AND HEALING

I am reminded of **Mark 5:26-30, She had suffered a great deal under the care of many doctors and had spent all she had, yet instead of getting better she grew worse. 27 When she heard about Jesus, she came up behind him in the crowd and touched his cloak, 28 because she thought, "If I just touch his clothes, I will be healed." 29 Immediately her bleeding stopped and she felt in her body that she was freed from her suffering.** Here a lady had bled for many years. People rejected her and scorned her because of her illness. In **John 10:10**, Jesus says, "**The thief does not come except to steal, and to kill, and to destroy. I have come that**

they may have life, and that they may have it more abundantly. "God has never lost a case and has the power to heal at any given time."

From a doctor's perspective, he treats and provides the medical treatment needed to heal. We know that God sustains us by placing people, professional people such as doctors, in our lives. The outcome of healing does not come from the doctors, but from God. In other words, doctors (men) treat, but God heals. How easy or hard for us to believe that? I will give you an example. In 1977, my maternal grandmother had open heart surgery and after surgery, she went into a coma. Every day was a struggle for the family seeing her lay there in a comatose state. I distinctly remember someone asking me about my grandmother's prognosis.

I spoke without hesitation and said, "She woke up today". That was with great hope and much faith because I believe he is a healer. There comes a time that all the praying and hoping does not work when at times there is a **but** in the equation of healing. I prayed and hoped that she would come out of her coma, but... God had other intentions.

When this lady, who had bled for many years, came to Jesus for healing, she was expecting only physical healing but, received much more. However, she received emotionally healing. Jesus healed her from the inside, first, to the outside. Let us look at this a little closer.

When reading scripture 28, it reads, **because she thought, "If I just touch his clothes, I will be healed** and 29 reads, **immediately her bleeding stopped, and she felt in her body that she was freed from her suffering.** Before this is explained further, allow me to add this scripture, **Proverbs 23:7** reads, **as a man thinketh in his heart, so is he.** Exactly when did the healing take place within this her? The healing begins in verse 28 because of her thinking and knowing that touching the hem of his garment would heal her was the beginning of her healing, emotionally. Perfect peace comes when our minds stay on Jesus but do remember that when we are ready to be healed, the devil will place a negative thought in your mind. God should always be our focus and daily target.

HAVING ALL HOPE FOR TOMORROW

The present and the past is known by all of us, but there is no one at this time that knows the future. If you knew what the future holds for you, what would you do about it?

We do not own crystal balls which further let us know that we cannot see into the future. Our time of death, gaining wealth, who and when we will marry are the things we will never know.

But why would we? The different journey that God takes us always has motives to follow. Our knowing the future possibilities would defeat the purpose for God being in our lives or being in existence. If we knew every facet of our lives, it would take the spice out of learning to grow in a spiritual manner, love unconditionally, recognize, and learn from our past mistakes.

In addition, if we are not able to sufficiently cope or comprehend with the problems within the present, how can we coherently deal with anything we can see in the future? Our lives would be so complex and overwhelmed and cognitively, we would not survive. Why? Because the goal in having hope is not knowing the future. That is why we have him.

So, it is imperative that we maintain the hope that God has instilled within us. Keep faith and lean strongly on God's promises and plan. His motives are lessons and teachings we are to take and apply to our everyday lives. Thus, we will have so much to share among others, especially our children. **Matthew 6:33-34** reminds us that we need to: **"33. But seek first his kingdom and his righteousness, and all these things will be given to you as well. 34 Therefore do not worry about tomorrow, for tomorrow will worry about itself. Each day has enough trouble of its own"**. In other words, we must take one step at a time as God will do the rest. We can only save us and we do not have any control of what takes place tomorrow or the day after.

Conclusion

God has given us the opportunity to make the choices that are pleasing to him. We need to be more content with the journey he has planned for each of us. But for our spiritual guide to take us to any level, we must be able to accept the general idea of what God expects of us and what we can expect from Him and that is He has all power to protect our worries and all our cares. We, by no means, are capable of pursuing anything that requires the expertise of God. We must maintain faith, look within ourselves (mirror), accept the special made journey He planned and do not allow anyone to dictate the position of your feelings. Lastly, we must maintain hope even through any disastrous situation and know that the outcome is worked by the will of God whether we approve or not. Do not dictate to Him of what we want. Trust the process as His greatness unfolds.

A Closing Prayer

Our heavenly Father. We come to you as humble as
we know how
Lord, give us the ability to pray when our hearts and
souls will not allow
Give us wisdom to look within our own souls
and lessen our grudgeful hearts to hurt others
Instill peace as we battle the storms you set for
us and help
us to understand that all things you have preceded before us
is for our good
And Lord as we grow, help us to grow with faith, love,
and conviction
Please do not allow us to make excuses for our
discrepancies
but give us insight to look to you to help battle the
unknown in this world

A Journey Towards God

In closing Lord, continue to provide the different
journey you have deemed
so that we may grow faithfully in you
All these things we ask in your son Jesus name
AMEN